# Sick as a Parrot!

by Steve Barlow and Steve Skidmore

Illustrated by Roger Langridge
Series Editors: Steve Barlow and Steve Skidmore

Published by Ginn and Company
Halley Court, Jordan Hill, Oxford OX2 8EJ
A division of Reed Educational and Professional Publishing Ltd
Telephone number for ordering **Impact**: 01865 888084

OXFORD   MELBOURNE   AUCKLAND   JOHANNESBURG
BLANTYRE   GABORONE   IBADAN   PORTSMOUTH (NH)
USA   CHICAGO

© Steve Barlow and Steve Skidmore 1999
The moral rights of the authors have been asserted.

All rights reserved. No part of this publication may be reproduced in any material form (including photocopying or storing it in any medium by electronic means and whether or not transiently or incidentally to some other use of this publication) without the prior written permission of the copyright owner, except in accordance with the provisions of the Copyright, Designs and Patents Act 1988 or under the terms of a licence issued by the Copyright Licensing Agency Ltd, 90 Tottenham Court Road, London W1P 9HE. Applications for the copyright owner's written permission to reproduce any part of this publication should be addressed in the first instance to the publisher.

First published 1999

2003  2002  2001  2000

10 9 8 7 6 5 4 3 2

ISBN 0 435 21263 X

*Illustrations*
Roger Langridge / Sylvie Poggio Artists Agent

*Cover artwork*
Roger Langridge / Sylvie Poggio Artists Agent

Designed by Shireen Nathoo Design

Printed and bound in Great Britain by Thomson Litho Ltd

# Contents

| | |
|---|---|
| Team Programme: Meet the Players! | 4 |
| Scene One | 8 |
| Scene Two | 21 |
| Scene Three | 33 |
| Scene Four | 42 |

# Crumbly United FC

## Team Programme

### Meet the Players!

**Today's match: Crumbly United v. Down Town**

### Chips Fraser

**Fact File**

*Position:* Goalkeeper
*Appearances*: 67
*Clean sheets*: 0

- Useless on crosses.
- Useless at diving.
- Useless at stopping shots.
- Useless at football, full stop! (Very good at eating.)

## Smoocher Harris

### Fact File

*Position*: Defender
*Appearances*: For Crumbly United – 87
 In court – 43

The bad boy of Crumbly United. Smoocher has a girl at every ground. He used to run 100 metres in 12 seconds, then he discovered girls. Now he couldn't run 12 metres in 100 seconds!

## C.D. Ron

### Fact File

*Position*: Striker
*Appearances*: 147
*Goals*: 3 (2 own goals)

Mad about computer games. Too many late night games sessions mean that C.D. can barely keep his eyes open on the pitch.

## Bikeshed Bob*

### Fact File

*Position*: Midfield
*Appearances*: Through the smoke.

Bob is not expected to line up with the team today. He'll probably be round the back of the changing rooms, as usual.

*Bikeshed Bob is not seen in the play. Only his cough and wheeze can be heard, and his smoke can be seen.

## Kevin Keystone

### Fact File

*Manager*
*Record*: Games played: 215
- Won: 0
- Drawn: 0
- Lost: 215
- Goals for: 6
- Goals against: 3,655

Sacked by all his previous clubs less than a week after taking charge. Kevin has taken on the worst manager's job in the history of the game. He says he'll lose each game as it comes.

# ... and meet the fan!

## Carol

**Fact File**

Chips' sister, Carol. Smoocher has been after Carol for ages, but she's been going out with someone else. Men fancy her – and she knows it!

## Next match: Crumbly United v. Barking Rovers

# Scene One

*The Crumbly United FC changing rooms. Dirty football kits hang from pegs and the floor is covered with muddy football boots. Chips, Smoocher and C.D. are sitting around in dirty kit, looking unhappy.*

SMOOCHER: It's not fair. Everyone else has got changed. Why can't we?

CHIPS: I'm hungry.

SMOOCHER: You're always hungry.

C.D. RON: *(In shock)* Twenty-six nil!

CHIPS: Oh come on, C.D., it's not that bad …

| | |
|---|---|
| C.D.: | *(Staring at him)* What could be worse than losing twenty-six nil? |
| CHIPS: | Losing twenty-seven nil? |
| C.D.: | Ha ha. |
| SMOOCHER: | I still don't see why we can't get changed. |
| CHIPS: | The boss said he wanted to see us. |
| SMOOCHER: | The boss? You mean Kevin? Nobody calls him 'the boss'. |
| CHIPS: | He likes us to call him boss. |
| SMOOCHER: | He likes us to win football matches, but we don't do that either. And why? Because our manager is a complete div! |

*(Kevin Keystone, the United manager, enters.)*

| | |
|---|---|
| KEVIN: | I heard that! *(Sarcastically.)* Who was it who kicked the ball into his own net? Me, or you? |

SMOOCHER: It was a back pass. *(He points at Chips.)* He dived the wrong way!

CHIPS: What?!

KEVIN: Both times?

SMOOCHER: My foot slipped the second time. Listen, Kevin…

KEVIN: I've told you to call me boss.

SMOOCHER: Yeah, right, Kevin. Can we get changed now? I've got to meet Sharon …

KEVIN: That's my point!

SMOOCHER: Eh?

C.D.: What is?

KEVIN: Crumbly United is the worst team in the league, and our worst players are you four… Hang on a minute. *(He counts them.)* There's only three of you. Where's Bob?

C.D.: Outside.

KEVIN: *(Sighs)* I don't believe it.

*(Kevin opens the door to the outside. A cloud of smoke drifts in. As Kevin talks to Bob, the smoke keeps pouring in. Bob replies in coughs instead of words.)*

KEVIN: Bob? Is that you?

| | |
|---|---|
| BOB: | *(Coughs once.)* |
| KEVIN: | Yes, I thought it was. What are you doing out there? |
| BOB: | *(Coughs once.)* |
| KEVIN: | Well, put it out. It'll stunt your growth. How many have you had today? |
| BOB: | *(Coughs and coughs and coughs.)* |
| KEVIN: | All right, don't go mad. How many have you had since full-time? |
| BOB: | *(Coughs six times.)* |
| KEVIN: | Six? The match only finished ten minutes ago. Finish that one and I'll talk to you later. |

*(Kevin shuts the door. The smoke stops.)*

| | |
|---|---|
| KEVIN: | Now, where was I? |
| SMOOCHER: | Moaning. |

| | |
|---|---|
| KEVIN: | Oh, yes! You four are the worst players in the team. And do you know why? |
| CHIPS: | No. Why? |
| KEVIN: | I'll tell you why! Because you've got no self-control! |
| CHIPS: | Eh? |
| KEVIN: | I mean look at you! Chips Johnson. The only man in football history who eats chips during a game! |
| CHIPS: | It was at half-time. I was hungry. And it was only a small bag. |

KEVIN: *(TO C.D.)* And what about you? C.D. Ron, the striker who needs a detective to find the goal for him. And why?

C.D.: Why?

KEVIN: You play too many computer games! You're up all hours fiddling with your joystick …

*(Smoocher sniggers.)*

KEVIN: *(To Smoocher)* And you can shut up, Smoocher Harris! All you think about is girls, girls, girls.

SMOOCHER: And girls.

KEVIN: I said shut it! You're all useless! I've decided it's time to take action. The rest of the lads agree with me. You're all going to have to give up the things you love.

| | |
|---|---|
| C.D., Chips and Smoocher: | *(Together)* WHAT?! |
| Kevin: | Chips, you're going on a diet … |
| Chips: | Me? No way! |
| Kevin: | C.D., you are not going to play any more computer games … |
| C.D.: | Bummer! |
| Kevin: | And as for you, Smoocher … no more girls! |
| Smoocher: | You've got to be kidding! *(He brushes back his hair.)* What are all those poor girls going to do without me? |

| | |
|---|---|
| KEVIN: | A lot better. Now listen. We've got a big match in two weeks. |
| CHIPS: | We know. Barking Rovers. In the Cup. |
| KEVIN: | Right. So no more chips, computer games or girls. You are going to give them all up for the next two weeks. Because if you don't, that's it! |
| SMOOCHER: | What's it? |
| KEVIN: | You'll be dropped. |

| | |
|---|---|
| C.D.: | *(In a horrified whisper)* Dropped! |
| CHIPS: | *(Shocked)* Dropped. |

SMOOCHER: Nobody's ever been dropped from Crumbly United. Not even Mad Dan Duncan who wore his boots on his hands.

KEVIN: Exactly! You'd never play football in this town again.
CHIPS: Oh, Kevin!
KEVIN: But I'm a fair man. Harsh, but fair. So, I'm going to give you a bit of encouragement.
SMOOCHER: *(Sarcastically)* That's nice.
KEVIN: I've collected a fiver each off the other lads.
CHIPS: Seven fivers – that's thirty-five quid!

KEVIN: And I'll put a fiver in myself. *(He brings out a wad of notes and adds another.)* That makes it forty quid. If you all hold out for two weeks, it's yours to share. If two of you make it, you can split it between you.

SMOOCHER: And if just one of us makes it, he gets the lot?
KEVIN: Right.
CHIPS: We'll do it!

SMOOCHER: All right lads. You know what they say. *(He holds a hand out, palm down.)* One for all …

CHIPS AND
C.D.: *(Putting their hands out, saying together)* … and all for one!

SMOOCHER: *(Pulls his hand away)* And every man for himself! Last one in the showers is a cream doughnut!

CHIPS: *(Dribbling)* Cream doughnut!

C.D.: *(Grabs Chips by the arms)* Come on!

*(C.D., Chips and Smoocher barge out through the door.)*

KEVIN: *(Shouting after them)* Just remember, no grub, no games, no girls!

*(Kevin opens the door. There is another blast of smoke.)*

KEVIN: And no more of that, right Bob?

BOB: *(Coughs once.)*

KEVIN: Okay, you can finish the packet first!

*(Kevin shuts the door.)*

KEVIN: I wonder if the England manager has this trouble!

# Scene Two

*In the sitting room in Chips Johnson's house, a few days later.*

(*Chips rushes in with one hand over his eyes.*)

CHIPS: No! No! You dirty, rotten … no! Aaaaargh!
(*Chips trips and falls onto the floor. Smoocher and C.D. follow more slowly. Smoocher holds a cake box tied with a ribbon. C.D. gives a horrible laugh. Smoocher kneels over Chips.*)

SMOOCHER: You know what we've got in the box, don't you?

(Chips shakes his head quickly. Smoocher slowly unties the box and opens it.)

SMOOCHER: Yes, you do. You know what's in here. You can smell them. You can taste them. You want them. *(He peers into the open box.)* Oh! Ohhhhhhhhh, yummmmm …

(C.D. and Smoocher each take a cream cake from the box and eat them to torment Chips.)

CHIPS: Have mercy!

(C.D. and Smoocher make 'yum-yum' noises. Chips tries to cover his eyes and ears at the same time.)

CHIPS: I'm not looking! I'm not listening! La-la-la-la …

*(C.D. and Smoocher lick the cream cakes with moans of delight. Then Smoocher's mobile phone rings. Smoocher answers it.)*

SMOOCHER: Hello? Oh, Sharon, hi. *(A pause.)* Oh, nothing much. We've just come round to Chips' house. We're trying to cheer him up.

*(Chips wails.)*

SMOOCHER: So how's my little darling tonight? What's that? You want me to come round? Now?

*(Smoocher suddenly realises that C.D. has stopped eating and Chips has stopped wailing. Both are watching him like hawks.)*

SMOOCHER: Er … um … oh, I dunno, it's a bit late. I've just washed my hair. Yeah, I know I've not seen you all week. I've been … Hello? Hello? She hung up!

(Smoocher bangs at the phone keys to try and reconnect with Sharon's number. C.D. takes a hand-held computer game out of his pocket.)

CHIPS: What are you doing?

C.D.: Oh, come on, Chips. It's only a small game.

CHIPS: No chance. Give it here.

SMOOCHER: *(Into the phone)* Hello? Hello? Sharon? Listen, I can explain. *(A pause.)* No, of course there isn't ... Hello? Hello, Sharon?

*(C.D. and Chips fight for the computer game.)*

CHIPS: Let go!

SMOOCHER: *(In a daze)* She thinks I'm seeing another woman.

*(Smoocher dials again. Chips manages to snatch C.D.'s game from him. C.D. immediately takes a different game out of another pocket and starts to play it.)*

C.D.: Gotta play ... gotta play ... kapow, zap! Die, alien scum ...

SMOOCHER: Sharon? Sharon, sweetheart – I swear there's no one else. Well, not at the moment, anyway ... Hello? Hello?

*(Chips snatches C.D.'s game.)*

CHIPS: Got it!

*(C.D. immediately fishes out yet another game.)*

C.D.: Daddy's been away, baby. Did you miss daddy?

CHIPS: *(To Smoocher)* I need back-up!

(Smoocher drops his mobile. He and Chips take C.D.'s games away from him. They all end up in a tangled heap on the sofa. Chips pulls away and smoothes his clothes down.)

CHIPS: Will you look at us? What's happened to us? Have we all gone mad?

C.D.: Sorry, guys. I guess I went a little crazy there.

SMOOCHER: I've lost Sharon. She was special. I really loved her. I've been going out with her for *days*.

C.D.: *(To Chips)* You're right. *(To Smoocher.)* He's right. We're being stupid.

(During the following speech, C.D. sneaks out of the room.)

SMOOCHER: Look, let's make a promise, right? No more getting at each other, no more crafty sneaking off for a snack …

CHIPS: Or a smooch.

SMOOCHER: Right. We've got to trust each other, haven't we C.D.? C.D.?

CHIPS: He's gone!

*(Chips and Smoocher gaze and each other, horror-stricken.)*

CHIPS AND
SMOOCHER: *(Together)* The Arcade!

*(Chips and Smoocher dash for the door, just as Chips' sister, Carol, comes in. Chips goes out but Smoocher stops as if he's run into a brick wall.)*

SMOOCHER: Oh, Carol. Hi!

CAROL: Where's my stupid brother off to?

SMOOCHER: He … er … I … er …

CAROL: I don't care really. *(She eyes up Smoocher.)* They call you Smoocher, don't they? They say you're a great kisser.

SMOOCHER: Yeah, do you want a demo? *(In a panic.)* No, no, sorry, forget I said that …

CAROL: What's the matter. Don't you like me?
SMOOCHER: No, no, it's not that. I think you're very … I mean, I thought you were going out with Thingy …
CAROL: I was. I ditched him.
SMOOCHER: Really? I mean … well, I've fancied you for ages but you never looked at me because you were with Thingy …
CAROL: Well, I'm not with Thingy now, am I?
SMOOCHER: No.
CAROL: Well then.

*(Carol moves towards Smoocher. They are just about to go into a clinch when Chips runs in.)*

CHIPS: NOOOOO!

SMOOCHER:   *(Shocked)* What?!

CHIPS:   *(To Carol)* Leave him alone!

SMOOCHER:   Push off, Chips! Sorry, Carol …

CAROL:   *(Her nose in the air)* Oh, that's all right. I expect you've got a nice game to play with my little brother. Come back and see me again – when you've grown up a bit.

*(Carol sweeps out. Smoocher stares longingly after her.)*

SMOOCHER:   Carol … Carol!

CHIPS: That was a lucky escape for you, mate. You were nearly tempted there.

SMOOCHER: I'm gonna kill you!

*(Smoocher reaches for Chips' throat as C.D. bursts in.)*

C.D.: Guys, you gotta lend me some money. There's some girl called Debbie in the Arcade. She's just beaten my best score on my all-time favourite game. I've got to get more than her. Lend me the money!

*(Chips and Smoocher look at each other. Then they look at C.D.)*

C.D.: What? Why are you looking at me like that?

*(Chips and Smoocher make a dive for C.D. They pile into the sofa and tip it backwards as they fight.)*

# Scene Three

*Match day. The Crumbly United changing rooms. C.D. is sitting, wearing football kit. He is playing with an imaginary game and making little computer game noises to himself. Smoocher and Chips enter. They are also wearing football kit. Smoocher is holding a blanket very tightly and stroking it. Chips staggers to a bench. He is thinner and shaking from lack of food.*

CHIPS: I feel all wobbly. I've got to sit down. Food … food …

SMOOCHER: Will you get a grip! *(Strokes his blanket.)* Carol, I can touch your hair ... I can feel your lips ...

*(Smoocher kisses the blanket passionately.)*

CHIPS: Oh, gross! Will you get rid of that thing!
SMOOCHER: It's all I have to remind me of Carol.
CHIPS: It didn't belong to Carol! It was her dog's blanket. You nicked it out of its kennel!
SMOOCHER: Well, she stroked the dog and the dog lay on the blanket. It's close enough. Anyway, I washed it.

CHIPS: Look at poor old C.D. He hasn't spoken a word since last Tuesday.

SMOOCHER: Look at us! We're all complete wrecks. I thought the idea of giving things up was to make us fit.

CHIPS: I've never felt less fit in my life. I keep having dizzy spells.

*(There is a knock at the door.)*

CHIPS: I hope that's food out there, because I'm going to eat it!

*(Kevin enters, glowing with pride in his team.)*

KEVIN: Are you ready to join the rest of the lads? You guys are looking mega-fit!

SMOOCHER: Kevin, we're knackered!

KEVIN: That's just nerves. You've got to say to yourselves, 'I am a lean, mean fighting machine'.

CHIPS AND
SMOOCHER: *(Together, glumly)* I am a lean, mean fighting machine.

C.D.: Peeeow! F'tang! Blip blip blip blip … zowie!

KEVIN: I think we'll take that as read. Where's Bob?

SMOOCHER: Outside.

*(Kevin opens the door, bracing himself for a blast of smoke. None appears.)*

KEVIN: Bob? Are you out there?

BOB: *(Wheezes horribly.)*

KEVIN: You look a bit strange. Are you sure you haven't been smoking?

BOB: *(Wheezes and laughs insanely.)*

KEVIN: You've been drinking coffee instead? How much have you had?

BOB: *(Wheezes three times.)*

KEVIN: Three cups? Well, that's not so bad …

BOB: *(Wheezes.)*

KEVIN: Three jars? You must be in orbit!

*(Bob wheezes. There is the sound of a body falling down.)*

KEVIN: Er ... good thinking, Bob, you have a lie down. In the mud. Keep yourself fresh, you can go on and murder them in the second half.

(Kevin shuts the door.)

SMOOCHER: Kevin, we can't play football! Look at Chips.

CHIPS: *(Staring ahead, he speaks feebly)* Why is it so dark? Mummy? Is that a burger I see before me?

KEVIN: Shape up, soldiers! You listen to me. Two weeks ago, you were human wrecks.

*(In the background, a recording of* Nessun Dorma, *the Italia '90 World Cup theme, begins to play. The music gets louder through Kevin's speech as he gets carried away.)*

KEVIN: You were weak and feeble. You had no self-control. Then you all gave up the things you loved the most. It hurt. It was tough. But you did it. Your bodies are pure. Your minds are razor-sharp.

*(Slowly, Chips, Smoocher and C.D. stop looking sorry for themselves. They stand up proudly.)*

KEVIN: Okay men, I want you to go out there and play. Play for your lives. Play until your lungs burst and your hearts break. You are tough!

C.D., CHIPS AND
SMOOCHER: *(Together)* We are tough!

KEVIN: You are strong!

C.D., CHIPS AND
SMOOCHER: *(Together)* We are strong!

KEVIN: You are not men. You are tigers!

C.D., CHIPS AND
SMOOCHER: *(Together)* We are tigers.

KEVIN: What are you?

C.D., CHIPS AND

SMOOCHER: *(Together)* We are tigers!

KEVIN: I can't hear you! **What are you?**

C.D., CHIPS AND

SMOOCHER: *(Roaring together)* **We are tigers!**

*(C.D., Chips and Smoocher rush out, roaring their battle cry. The music builds to a climax. Kevin watches them go, punching the air in victory.)*

# Scene Four

*Two hours later, in the Crumbly United changing rooms. Kevin is waiting for his team.*

(C.D., Chips and Smoocher stumble in. They are bruised, they are muddy, they are tired out. They limp to seats and sit in silence for a moment.)

KEVIN: Boys, boys, boys. You were terrific out there today! You were *numero uno*, on the money, out-of-sight mega mind-blowing perfecto! I am over the moon!

SMOOCHER: Kevin, we lost.

KEVIN: So?

SMOOCHER: Kevin, we lost fifteen-nil!

KEVIN: And your point is?

C.D.: Kevin, I think what Smoocher is trying to say is that we gave up computer games …

| | |
|---|---|
| CHIPS: | *(With longing)* And food … |
| SMOOCHER: | *(In a trance)* And girls … |
| C.D.: | We put ourselves through hell because you told us we would be better players if we showed a bit of self-discipline. And what happened? |
| SMOOCHER: | We were pants. |
| CHIPS: | We sucked. |

C.D.: And we lost fifteen-nil. Now, call me Mister Picky, but I don't think this is the result we were all hoping for.

KEVIN: Okay, so you lost fifteen-nil. But last time, you lost twenty-six-nil. So this time, you lost by eleven goals fewer than you did last time!

*(C.D., Chips and Smoocher stare at Kevin.)*

CHIPS: Does anybody mind if I just curl up somewhere and die?

KEVIN: And this is only the beginning! Wait until you see what I've got lined up before the next game.

SMOOCHER: *(Dangerously)* What?

KEVIN: An all-lettuce diet, sessions on the army assault course …

CHIPS: Kevin …

KEVIN: And a few hours at the health club.

SMOOCHER: We can't afford the health club!

KEVIN: It's all right lads. The forty quid just covered it …

CHIPS: What forty quid?

KEVIN: Your winnings. I knew you wouldn't mind.

C.D.: We do mind!

KEVIN: Then there's weight training, Turkish baths, yoga …

*(C.D., Chips and Smoocher hurl football kit at Kevin until he collapses in a heap.)*

CHIPS: Anyone coming down the chip shop?

C.D.: Only if we can stop off at the Arcade. Coming, Smoocher?

SMOOCHER: No thanks. I'm going out to find a girl. In fact, I'm going out to find three girls.

*(Chips kneels beside Kevin.)*

CHIPS: Are you still over the moon, Kev?

*(Kevin kneels up. He spits out a sock. He mumbles something.)*

C.D.: What did he say?

Chips: I think he said, he's as sick as a parrot.

C.D. and Smoocher: *(Together)* Result!

## SET A

**It's Only an Animal**
by Frances Usher

**Runaway**
by Jeremy Davies

## SET B

**Star Bores**
by Steve Barlow and Steve Skidmore

**Top of the Mops**
by Julia Donaldson

## SET C

**The Big Time**
by Jean Ure and Leonard Gregory

**The Weekend War**
by Tony Bradman

**Sick as a Parrot**
by Steve Barlow and Steve Skidmore

**The Half Monty**
by John Townsend

## SET D

**Honest**
by Jon Blake

**The Shadow**
by Ritchie Perry

**Arcade Games**
by Jon Blake

**Beware the Wolf**
by Alan Dapré